Decauville Band

White Dream Journey
The book

Piano/Vocal Sheet Music

by Argyris Lazou

Decauville Band

White Dream Journey

The book

Piano/Vocal Sheet Music

by Argyris Lazou

Art work & Drawings

By Dimitra Xenaki

Copyright 2017 Argyris Lazou. All rights reserved.
Unauthorized Duplication is a violation of applicable laws.

Printed by CreateSpace, An Amazon.com Company

Made in U.S.A.

ISBN 978-960-93-9040-8

Contents

4
Red Sky

9
Happy Old Child

13
Promised Land

18
White Dream

25
Night Breeze

27
Suzy

30
This Is Love

34
Bacchic dance

38
Masks

39
Biographies

Red Sky — Lyrics by D. Xenaki

Love is a garden of flowers
N' you choose to pick up sadness
When you just know
that life's too short

There is no point to regret
You know life has its own wisdom
Just try to find your way to freedom

Red Sky
Let's fly
Get away n' drink sweet wine
If you don't know
which way to choose
Keep going and laugh at time

We are born in tears and pain
N' the choices look so vain
When the crossway is lost
in haze and rain

Just find the strength to forgive
And only love will show you a light
When you will be left
alone in the night

Red Sky
Let's fly
Get away n' drink sweet wine
If you don't know
which way to choose
Keep going and laugh at time

Red Sky
Let's fly
Get away n' drink sweet wine
If you don't know
which way to choose
Have fun and laugh at time

Red Sky
Let's fly
Get away n' drink sweet wine
If you don't know
which way to choose
Keep going and laugh at time

Red Sky
Let's fly
Get away n' drink sweet wine
If you don't know
 which way to choose
Have fun and laugh at time

If you don't know
which way to choose
Keep going and laugh at time

If you don't know
which way to choose
Have fun and laugh at time

If you don't know
which way to choose
Keep going and laugh at time

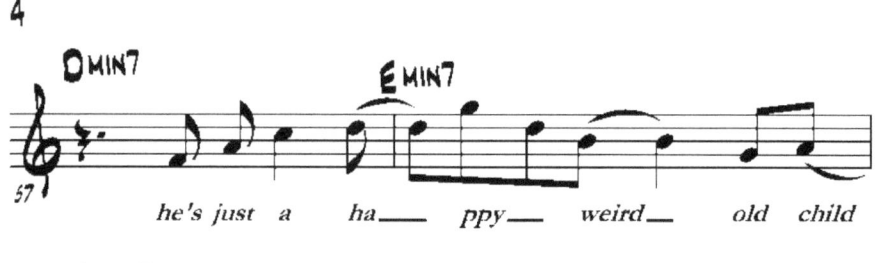

Happy Old Child Lyrics by D. Xenaki

He is such a lonely dreamer
Drifting all alone
Drinks a lot at bar at nights
Sitting all night long

You know you will
never see him crying
He is a happy, weird, old child

In his mind he has created
Such a dreamy world
But he is so brave to face life
And always say a good word

We are scared of time
but he never minds
He is a happy, weird, old child

He will buy a drink if you need
Someone to speak
With an open heart he will hear you
Nothing makes him freak

He doesn't judge or criticize
His love is made of Paradise
He is a happy, weird, old child

We are scared of time
but he never minds
He is a happy, weird, old child
He' s just a happy, weird, old child

Always walks alone

Promised Land   Lyrics by D. Xenaki

Behind the sun you hide your face
I have no life for years
Though dust has covered your last trace
I think that you are still here

Love is a dreamy experience
Like the way children draw
In the streets of lost innocence
I am looking for you now

I remember of the days
We used to laugh and play
There's nothing more to say

I remember of the days
We were kissing on the sand
Oh! What a Promised Land

Now I can feel that is all that clear
Needs courage to forgive
The echo of love still sounds here
I have much more to give

I remember of the days
We used to laugh and play
There's nothing more to say

I remember of the days
We were kissing on the sand
Oh! what a Promised Land

I remember of the days
We used to laugh and play
There's nothing more to say

I remember of the days
We were kissing on the sand
Oh! What a Promised Land

I remember of the days

We used to have it all

Just our Promised Land

White Dream Lyrics by D. Xenaki

I'm a flame, can you feel it?
Your butterfly in rain
All lost dreams can be seen now
In your eyes babe

Taste the light in a breath now
N' feel the bright new dawn
All in life seems to be vain
Now but love

Close your eyes
N' I'll be right here
Paradise
Is my gift for you

White dream
 There's no shadow
Only time to dream
In the dark I will bring you rainbows
In angels' gardens

Taste the light in a kiss now
N' feel the bright new dawn
All in life seems to be vain
Now but love

Close your eyes
N' I'll be right here
Paradise
Is my gift for you

Hold me tight
Turn in joy any fear
One way flight
To the sun with no doubt

Close your eyes
N' I'll be right here
Paradise
Is my gift for you

Hold me tight
Turn in joy any fear
One way flight
To the sun with no doubt

Close your eyes
N' I'll be right here
Paradise
Is my gift for you

Suzy   Lyrics by D. Xenaki

Suzy Suzy where are you this evening
Suzy Suzy you never sleep alone
Suzy Suzy you will get
burned some day like a cheap lover babe
In the flames of love

Suzy Suzy where are you this evening
Suzy Suzy you never sleep alone
Suzy Suzy you will get
burned some day like a cheap lover babe in
the flames of love

You asked for his love
You have got all
Don't know what you want
You are just bored

You have lost your way
Born to betray
You've nothing to say
He was just yours

Suzy Suzy where are you this evening
Suzy Suzy you never sleep alone
Suzy Suzy you will get
burned some day like a cheap lover babe
In the flames of love

Suzy Suzy where are you this evening
Suzy Suzy you never sleep alone
Suzy Suzy you will get
burned some day like a cheap lover babe
In the flames of love

You broke his heart
You drove him nuts
N' you know what?
Never come back

You treated him bad
He ain't your toy
And I know it is hard
to say you are sorry

Suzy Suzy where are you this evening
Suzy Suzy you never sleep alone
Suzy Suzy you will get
burned some day like a cheap lover babe
In the flames of love

Suzy Suzy where are you this evening
Suzy Suzy you never sleep alone
Suzy Suzy you will get
burned some day like a cheap lover babe
In the flames of love

COPYRIGHT 2017   ARGYRIS LAZOU

This is Love   Lyrics by D. Xenaki

Among the traces
I can make out your own
in the rain
Your love is a sun
That can wash away all my pain

Inside your kiss
My old soul takes a deep breath
N' in your arms
My Spirit has been
recovered from death

Now I think I'm just reborn
N' all I lived and I knew before
Now I think all lay behind the truth

Take me
Show me how to fly
Even when the flowers die
Take me
Far above
This is love

When leaves are withered
I think about you and
my soul does sing
You give me fever
My body now is dust in the wind

Inside a dream
You have got me just
resurrected in light
I'm your sunbeam
Your angel born spark in the night

Now I feel I'm just reborn
N' all I lived and I knew before
Now I think all all behind the truth

Take me
Show me how to fly
Even when the flowers die
Take me Far above
This is love

Take me
Show me how to fly
Even when the flowers die
Take me
Far above
This is love

Seize me
Make me numb and melt
Taste pure immortal sweat
Take me far above
This is love

Inside your kiss
My old soul takes a deep breath
N' in your arms
My Spirit has been
recovered from death…

Bacchic Dance   Lyrics by D. Xenaki

I can smell in your fragrance
You are made of fire
In your eyes is shining
Such a wild child

A witch's wish has blessed you
With a magic kiss
In the dark
You transform me
In a flaming spark
In a flaming spark

I wanna shake you babe
We only live just once
Come on light up the night
In such a bacchic dance
In such a bacchic dance

When you touch me my cells
Turn into stars
Wild angel
Sweet danger
You just drive me nuts

A witch's wish has blessed you
With a magic kiss
In the dark
You transform me
 in a flaming spark
In a flaming spark

I wanna shake you babe
We only live just once
Come on light up the night
In such a bacchic dance
In such a bacchic dance

I wanna shake you babe
We only live just once
Come on light up the night
In such a bacchic dance
In such a bacchic dance

Red passion in your eyes
We only live just once
Now rain turns into wine
In such a bacchic dance
In such a bacchic dance

COPYRIGHT 2017 ARGYRIS LAZOU

MASKS

CHILL OUT

MUSIC BY A. LAZOU & L. GRIGORIAN
LYRICS BY DIMITRA XENAKI

Decauville Band

Argyris Lazou was born in Florina, in 1970. He studied Musicology in the Aristotle University of Thessaloniki and he also holds a degree in Piano and Theory of Music. At the age of fourteen he formed a hard rock band, called *Skyhooks*, performing in Northern Greece. Later he was occupied with jazz and ethnic jazz music. He is a Head Teacher in secondary education and has been working for several years as a Music Teacher.

Dimitra Xenaki was born in Athens, in 1984. She has a degree in Theatrical Studies, at the University of Athens and Fine Arts at the University of Western Macedonia. She has attended classes in electric guitar and vocals and has cooperated with hard rock bands as a vocalist and composer. She works as a visual arts and drama teacher.

Levon Grigorian was born in Yerevan, Armenia in 1965. He was the bassist of the band *New Rose* for several years, in the city of Thessaloniki. He is a teacher of music in double bass and electric bass at a Conservatory.

Elias Michailides was born in 1965, in Thessaloniki. He was the drummer of the bands *Mikro Band, New Rose* and he has also cooperated with vocalist Julie Massino. He teaches percussion at Drum Land Sound Music Academy.

Copyright 2017 Argyris Lazou. All rights reserved.
Unauthorized Duplication is a violation of applicable laws.

Printed by CreateSpace, An Amazon.com Company

Made in U.S.A.

ISBN 978-960-93-9040-8

www.ingramcontent.com/pod-product-compliance
Lightning Source LLC
Chambersburg PA
CBHW042127080426
42734CB00001B/23